THE SOMERSET LEVELS

Rodney Legg

First published in Great Britain in 2010

British Library Cataloguing-in-Publication Data
A CIP record for this title is available from the British Library

ISBN 978 1 906887 86 5

PiXZ Books
Halsgrove House, Ryelands Industrial Estate,
Bagley Road, Wellington, Somerset TA21 9PZ
Tel: 01823 653777
Fax: 01823 216796
email: sales@halsgrove.com

An imprint of Halstar Ltd, part of the Halsgrove group of companies
Information on all Halsgrove titles is available at: www.halsgrove.com

Printed and bound in China by Toppan Leefung Printing Ltd

Contents

How to use this book

The Area

The historic line of the Somerset coast in 7000 BC, off Hinkley Point, was three miles out into what is now Bridgwater Bay. Existing foreshore at Hinkley Point covers six beds of peat. The lowest of these (40 feet below present sea level) dates from the time when sea levels were rising after the end of the last Ice Age. Shoreline woods at Stolford were becoming a submerged forest by 3806 BC. That is a key date. Tree-ring analysis shows that Neolithic people were advancing into the wetlands, along what we know as the Sweet Track from firm ground at Shapwick, which is the oldest-known road in Europe.

Sea walls, causeways and drainage ditches date from the monastic period when ecclesiastical owners such as Glastonbury Abbey and Wells Cathedral required tenants to protect their investments. The next great move forward in land reclamation, reversing the inland surges of the sea, came with a raft of Inclosure Acts. Attempts to drain King's Sedgemoor were resisted by the commoners in 1775, 1788 and 1791, but a £60,000 project went forward in 1796. This enclosed 18,000 acres.

Out in the inter-tidal zone of the Bristol Channel, Brendan Sellick is the last of the mud fishermen. He pushes a mud-horse from Stolford to sets of vertical nets attached to stakes up to two miles offshore.

On land there is peat-digging, once for fuel and now for horticulture, and the willow is cropped for basket-making, cricket bats and bio-fuel. The most high-profile product from the Levels are baskets for hot-air balloons, made by the Hill family, from Bridgwater. Much of the worked-out peatlands are reverting back to nature in an extensive series of wildlife sanctuaries. Herons abound, the otter and the water vole are back, and great flocks of wintering duck and geese return each winter to Bridgwater Bay.

Gripes, gutters, ditches, rhynes, drains and rivers. These are the six stages of water management in the withy wetlands. Gripes and gutters flow into ditches and rhynes (named by 17th-century Dutch engineers for their home waterways) which join canal-sized man-made drains and canalised natural rivers.

The Routes

All routes are circular - meaning they bring you back to the starting point - and are of moderate length. They vary from four to nine miles and are graded from one to three boots - from easy to the more challenging. They are ideal for families or groups of friends looking for an afternoon in glorious historic countryside or for a more leisurely walk with a suitable pause at a pub or refreshment spot en route. None of the terrain is pushchair friendly, so back-pack the toddler.

Starting points are given with map references and postcodes, because the latter are necessary for some car-borne navigation systems.

Direction details specify compass points which, clockwise, are N (north), NNE (north-northeast), E (east), ESE (east-southeast), SE (south-east), SSE (south-southeast), S (south), SSW (south-southwest), SW (south-west), WSW (west-southwest), W (west), WNW (west-northwest), NW (north-west) and NNW (north-northwest). The general direction can be assumed to remain the same until another compass point is given. Carry a compass.

Routes are along public rights of way or across access land. Both categories may be subject to change or diversion. Remember that conditions under foot will vary greatly according to the season and the weather. Do not set off into the Levels when they are flooded.

Parking spaces are specified on the assumption that many walkers will arrive by car or bicycle. Where public transport is mentioned, there were options currently available, but check these with the provider before setting off. Ensure you find out the time of the last bus or train.

Maps

Though we give a self-contained potted description of each walk, our sketch maps can only be a rough guide. The Somerset Levels are covered on three OS sheets, Explorer Maps 140, 141 and 128 and their use is recommended.

Key to Symbols Used

Level of difficulty:

Easy ♥

Fair ♥♥

More challenging ♥♥♥

Map symbols:

 Park & start

Road

----- Track

.... Footpath

■ Building / Town

Pub

▲ Landmark

+ Church

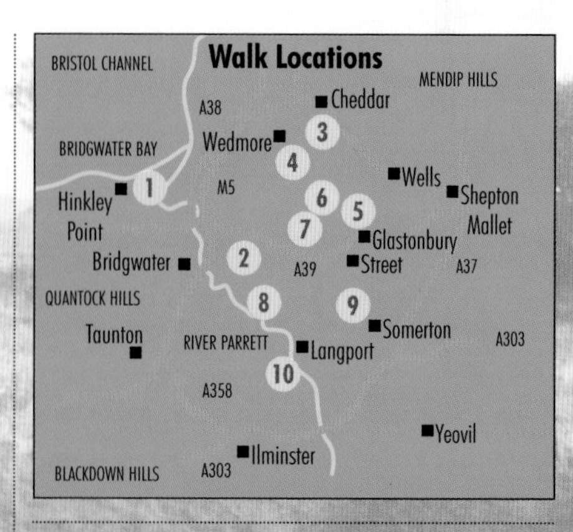

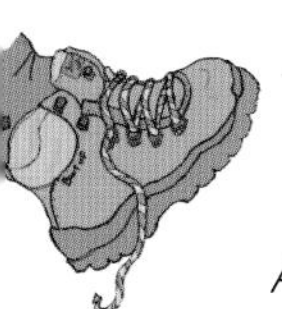

1 Stert Point and Bridgwater Bay

A 9-mile circuit around the peninsula where the Parrett meets the sea

Stert Island, beyond the hamlet of Steart - yes, they are spelt differently - is the ultimate seaward extremity of the Somerset Levels. Stert Point, with its wedge of coastal grassland and a timber tower for a bird hide and viewpoint, overlooks a wetland of thousands of acres of mud and reeds. The sea comes and goes, tidally, every 12 and a half hours. Winter is the best time for experiencing huge influxes of birds as flocks of ducks and geese desert their Arctic breeding grounds for a milder option on the Atlantic seaboard. As for time of day, if you have the choice, towards the top of a rising tide is ideal as the incoming water drives oystercatchers and waders ever closer to the peninsula that separates Bridgwater Bay from the Parrett estuary. The backdrop includes Hinkley Point nuclear power station and its water-cooling intake. This landmark becomes ever-closer, rising gaunt and austere. The walk also takes in the villages of Stockland Bristol (formerly owned by the city) and Otterhampton (which once again has otters in residence) plus the seaward end of the River Parrett.

Level:

Terrain: Low-lying, liable to muddy patches, and rhyne-crossing diversions.

Length: 9 miles

Park & start: In the **Bridgwater Bay National Nature Reserve** car-park which is a field on the left in the middle of **Steart** hamlet after **Quantock View Farm.**

Start ref.: ST 274 459

Postcode: TA5 2PX

Public transport: None

Websites: www.naturalengland.org.uk www.visitsomerset.co.uk

Tower Hide

Due to the funnelling effect of its estuary, the Bristol Channel experiences the second highest rise and fall of the tides in the world - by up to 42 feet - which is exceeded only by the Bay of Fundy in Canada.

(1) Set off along the cul-de-sac lane (NE) and pass **Dowells Farm**, **Collard Farm**, **Cox's Farm** and **Manor Farm**, in 500 metres. Here the road becomes a track. Follow it around to the right in 400 metres. Turn left in 100 metres. Enter grassland in 200 metres and bear right to **Tower Hide**, overlooking **Stert Point**, in a further 200 metres. Three smaller hides are much closer to the mud and the birds with a fourth overlooking a scrape.

Wall Common

(2) Turn towards Hinkley Point (W) and go through the gate in the corner of the field in 175 metres. Now follow the low ridge (SW) beside reedbeds to your right and the pastures of **Stert Flats** to the left. Pass the last of the farms, in 2,000 metres, and go through a gate into **Wall Common**. Continue to follow the shore to the sand dunes and the remains of a Second World War pillbox in 500 metres.

Hinkley Point from Catsford Common

3 Beyond we walk along a stretch of stony road (W), with a grassy causeway to the right, towards an ever-larger nuclear power station, looking increasingly gaunt, austere and Soviet, even. In 2,000 metres we pass a lagoon on the inshore side of the coastal causeway.

Established in 1954, by what was then the Nature Conservancy, Bridgwater Bay National Nature Reserve now has international accolades for its 20,000 waders, 50,000 wintering duck, 30,000 lapwing and 2,000 oystercatchers.

4 After the lagoon, in a further 300 metres, the farmland wall to the left turns inland. This is now **Catsford Common** with Stolford Farm beyond. Turn left down towards the kink in the wall (SW), in 150 metres, to the field gate 40 metres to the left of it.

5 Enter the farmland along a public footpath and bear right to the left-hand of the two gates towards the corner of the first pasture. Head to the left-hand (S) of another two gates and keep **Whitewick Farm** to your right in 400 metres.

Though it is almost at sea level, there is a panoramic view from the observation hide at Stert Point around the Parrett Estuary and Bristol Channel from Steep Holm, South Wales, Brean Down and Burnham-on-Sea inland to Brent Knoll, the Mendips Hills, Cheddar Gorge, West Huntspill, the Somerset Levels and around the Quantock Hills and Hinkley Point with Dunkery Beacon and Exmoor beyond to Hurlstone Point and the Atlantic Ocean.

Bridgwater Bay sand dunes

6 Then comes another gate, followed by the field to the left of the farm. Bear left but ignore the orchard gate. There are then two further gates in the left-hand hedgerow. Go through the first of these, with a hedgerow to the right, and through the farmstead in 350 metres.

7 Continue straight ahead, through the gate, towards the sag-point between the closest pair of pylons. Cross the stream in 300 metres and go through the gate in the corner of the next field, in 200 metres, after passing under the cables.

8 Walk up the slope to **Woolstone Farm** in 300 metres. The path goes to the right of the barns, through the yard, and turns right (W) beside the farmhouse. Then turn left (S) in 50 metres, through the field gates, with the frontage of the house to your left.

9 Proceed straight ahead across the pasture down to a foot-bridge, across **North Brook** in 250 metres, to the right of the telegraph pole and some scrubby trees. Continue across the meadows - admiring a dainty stone-arched bridge - and climb the slope, to the gate in 500 metres, beneath pine trees in the top corner of the field. The tower of **Stockland Bristol** Church is to the left and cupola of the **Old School** (now Stockland Sports Club) to the right.

A dainty stone-arched bridge

10 Turn left to the steps into the churchyard at **St Mary's** and then immediately right to cross the road to the garden gate. Pass to the left of the house in 100 metres and continue through the gate. Then turn left in 15 metres, across a stile in the hedgerow, beneath the electricity pole. Cross this field diagonally (SE) towards the church tower and house on the other side.
Go through the gate in a kink in the hedgerow to a footbridge midway along the dense lower hedgerow of this second arable field in 500 metres.

Parrett wetlands

North Clyce

11 Walk up the slope (S) and skirt the walled garden to the right of the house in 150 metres. Turn left (E) on the other side, through the field gate and down the lane into **Otterhampton**. Pass **All Saints' Church** in 250 metres.

12 Turn left (N), towards Steart, at the junction in 100 metres. Turn right (NE) at the next junction, after **Rose Cottage**, in 800 metres. This is **Steart Drove** (which you drove along earlier).

Stert Point and Stert Island lie beyond the hamlet of Steart in an area of so much tidal mud that twice every day there is more of the parish of Otterhampton under water than above it.

13 Turn right (SE) in 200 metres, through the field gate immediately after **South Brook**. A public footpath follows the water-course to **Combwich Clyce** where it enters the **River Parrett** in 1,500 metres.

14 Turn left (N), following the flood defences, to **North Clyce** in 1,200 metres. Here **North Brook** flows into the river. Continue straight ahead (NE) along the Parrett Trail, to re-enter the nature reserve, with reed-beds and expanses of mud. Look out at low tide for otter trails.

15 In 1,500 metres the coastal path approaches a pair of gates. Bear left down to the lower one and the stile beside it. Follow the unpaved farm road (N) into **Steart**, for 1,500 metres, to the lane opposite **Dowells Farm**. Turn left (W) to return to your car in 100 metres.

All Saints' at Otterhampton

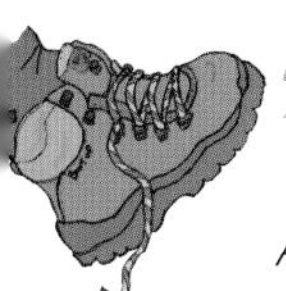

2 Westonzoyland and Sedgemoor

A 5-mile battlefield walk, linking landmarks with the misfortunes of the Duke of Monmouth

The Western Rebellion began on 11 June 1685 when James Scott, Duke of Monmouth, landed from Holland at Lyme Regis. He claimed the Stuart throne from his uncle, James II, in a popular Protestant uprising against an autocratic Catholic monarch. Militarily it was no contest. Poorly organised and weakly armed, 4,000 men attempted to creep up on 2,600 well-trained soldiers, during the night of Sunday 5 July. Things fell apart as a musket shot and a shout alerted the royal camp near Bussex Farm. Having lost the element of surprise the rebels were instantly out-manoeuvred. Up to 400 were killed during the action and 1,000 were summarily slaughtered later on 6 July. The Royalists lost 200 men.

Monmouth fled but was caught in Dorset, and beheaded on Tower Hill. Some 250 supporters were hanged, drawn and quartered in the Bloody Assize and 850 transported to the West Indies.

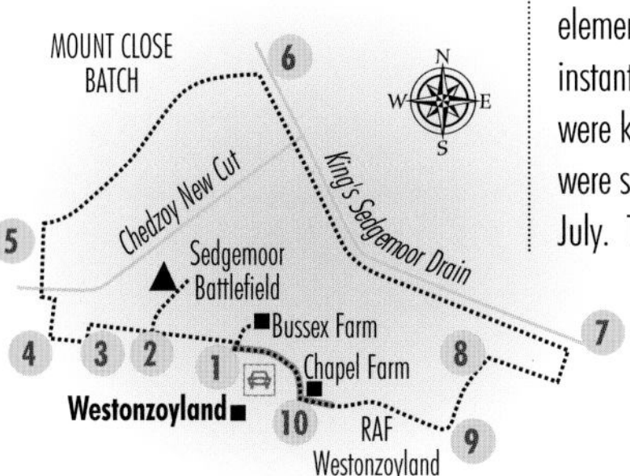

Level:

Length: 5 miles

Terrain: Four arable fields but otherwise along droveways, or across pastures, and just about flat though with stout stiles all along the flood plain.

Park & start: In the vicinity of **Somerset Willow Growers** at Bussex Farm which is reached by turning off the A372 at the western end of **Westonzoyland** (into **King's Road** then to the end of **Monmouth Road** at a 'No through road' sign in 1,200 metres).

Start ref.: ST 356 354

Postcode: TA7 0EU

Public transport: Buses from Bridgwater to Langport.

Websites: www.musgrovewillows.co.uk www.sedgemoor.gov.uk/westonzoyland

Bussex Farm

(1) Set off (W) down into the meadows from **Bussex Farm** to the junction of droveways in 600 metres. (Imagine and the royal cavalry and soldiers camped behind you in tents, out in the open, without any entrenchments.)

(2) Here we have a diversion to the right (NE) along **Langmoor Drove** for 600 metres - there and back - to see the Cornish granite memorial and cross the site of the **Battle of Sedgemoor**. (Visualise the rebels out here, exposed and in the open, wasting ammunition as they fired aimlessly for an hour in the dark towards the King's troops who were keeping their heads down around Bussex Farm. Conversely, Monmouth's cavalry failed to find a crossing through the rhyne and were shot off their horses by the King's men.)

Parish memorial to later war dead

(3) Our onward route, on returning to the junction of droveways, is to continue (W) towards Chedzoy. Follow this drove leftwards around the corner (S) in 300 metres.

Then turn right (W) at a gate in 100 metres. (There was an outlying detachment of 150 of the King's men in this vicinity on the night of 5-6 July 1685, so the rebels - who had marched out of Bridgwater - could not approach through Chedzoy.)

King's Sedgemoor Drain

4 Follow the hedge and power cables to the ditch in the corner of the arable field in 200 metres. Turn right (N) on the other side to **Chedzoy New Cut** in 300 metres. Turn left and then right to cross the footbridge. Proceed to **Moor Drove Rhyne** in 300 metres.

Chedzoy New Cut

5 Turn right (NE) along **Moor Drove**. Pass under the pylon line in 400 metres. Turn right on reaching a farm road beside **Mount Close Batch** in 700 metres. Approach **King's Sedgemoor Drain** in 400 metres.

Droveways across the Somerset Levels often have no apparent legal status but they were created by Act of Parliament for common access, without legal ownership, so no one has lawful authority to order you off them.

'Beat the drums, the enemy is come, for the Lord's sake beat the drums,' was the cry that raised the alarm in the royal camp at Bussex Farm in the early hours of 6 July 1685.

(Here, as Monmouth's men approached, they were spotted by a royal soldier who raised the alarm. The rebels had come from Peasey Farm - two miles to the left along the course of the canal-like 'drain' - but think of it as a contemporary lesser water-course known as Black Ditch.)

Sedgemoor memorial

6 Turn right (SE) along a grassy path across stiles beside the line of gates. This is across the flood plain with the water to your left and an embankment to the right. Water, path and bank bend to the left in 1,000 metres. Proceed along the waterside path for a further 1,000 metres.

Dakota transports with paratroops of United States 101st Airborne Division from RAF Westonzoyland began dropping near Sainte Mare Eglise in Normandy at 01.30 hours on 6 June 1944 to begin the D-Day offensive behind Utah Beach.

Battlefield rhyne

7 Turn right (SSW) on reaching **KSD Footbridge** (without crossing the water). Follow the ditch to the metal gates on the other side of the meadow in 200 metres. Turn right (NNW) along **Sedgemoor Drove**. Burdenham Farm is to the left in 150 metres. Proceed straight ahead, through the gate, and continue to a footpath sign in 300 metres.

The Sedgemoor Inn

8 Turn left (SSW) through a kissing gate, across two meadows, to gates and stiles below the ridge and pillbox on the other side.

The Battle of Sedgemoor took place between Bussex Rhyne, Langmoor Rhyne and Black Ditch - with the Royal Army coming out of Westonzoyland and Monmouth's rebels moving across country - but the lie of the land was radically changed in the 18th century with the cutting of King's Sedgemoor Drain.

9 Go through the gates in 500 metres and then turn right (WNW) in 10 metres. Follow the grass strip between an arable field and the rhyne to a gate in 150 metres. Continue straight ahead up the slope along a grassy path through

Outlying hut at Liney

scrub on the edge of **Westonzoyland Aerodrome**. Keep the ruins of its scattered buildings to your left, and fields to your right, and exit along the former access road which heads towards bungalows at **Liney** in 1,000 metres.

10 Join **Liney Road** on a corner. Turn sharp right (NW), along the lesser lane, to pass **Chapel Farm** and **Hill View**. Return to **Sedgemoor House** and **Bussex Farm** in 500 metres.

Canberra PR7 bombers of the Atomic Trials Task Force took off from Westonzoyland for Australia in March 1956, to test nuclear weapons at Monte Bello and Maralinga.

Westonzoyland

3 Cheddar Moor and Nyland

An 9-mile circuit of the flat-lands below and beside the Mendip Hills

There is another Cheddar, out of town and away from the world-famous Gorge, which forms the northern extremity of the Somerset Levels. Cheddar Moor is crossed by a network of rhynes and rivers with a big round reservoir as the 20th-century addition to the landscape. Once drained, the peaty land was ploughed - wiping out traces of prehistoric occupation - though these days it is mostly pasture. En route are the historic hamlets of Clewer and Cocklake, on firmer ground, and a cluster of farmsteads around Nyland Hill which geologically is the oldest point in sight. Back in town, we pass the great tower of St Andrew's Church, which contains the bones and monuments of the Cheddars of Cheddar. Lesser treasures have been locked away. 'The only antique is the vicar,' proclaims a notice in the porch.

Cheddar
Cheddar Reservoir
Stubbington Drove
Puddleham Corner
River Axe
Broadmoor Drove
Notlake Farm
Clewer
Maldon Farm
Bartlett's Bridge
Nyland
Moor Mead Farm
Top Road
Bath Arms Hotel
1 2 3 4 5 6 7 8 9 10 11 12 13 14 15 16
N E S W

Level:
Length: 9 miles
Terrain: Long lengths of droves and lanes with one significant hill.
Park & start: From the car-park beside **Cheddar Reservoir** which is reached from the A371 via **Lower New Road** and **Sharpham Road** (through the gates at the far end beside Sharpham Road Playing Fields which also have a car-park).
Start ref.: ST 446 533
Postcode: BS27 3DR
Public transport: Buses from Axbridge to Wells.
Websites:
www.cheddarparishcouncil.org.uk
www.sedgemoor.gov.uk/cheddar.tic

Nyland bridleway

1 Set off through the kissing gate and up on to the embankment. Bristol Water allows public access. Turn left (W) with Cheddar behind you and the water and Axbridge to the right. Proceed around the rim of the lake, with great crested grebe and swallows in season, for 1,000 metres. On approaching this corner - if a circle can be said to have such a thing - there is a kink in the fence-line down to the left. Descend from point No. 78 on the wall to a stile beneath two oak trees to the left of a field gate.

The principal Cheddar altar-tomb is to Thomas de Cheddar (circa 1443) and the family's finest brass to a gowned Lady Isabella de Cheddar (died 1474).

2 Cross the anglers' car-park and then turn right (SW) along **Stubbington Drove**. Proceed straight ahead for 1,000 metres and cross the **Cheddar Yeo**. Also continue straight ahead on the other side (ignoring a second path to the left) to the **River Axe Intake** in 600 metres where we cross a bridge.

3 Turn left (SSE), through the field gate, and keep the **River Axe** to your left. Follow its bank around to the left (SE) at **Puddleham Corner** in 200 metres. In 500 metres, at a bridge, the path joins **Broadmoor Drove**. Continue straight ahead along the river-bank. Keep an eye out for herons along the lesser water-course, in **Lanham Rhyne**, to your right.

4 In 1,200 metres, pass Notlake Farm bungalow and then a pumping station, on the opposite bank. The drove now forks right (SSE), away from the river, to **Marlin Haven, Ragwood Farm** and into Clewer in 300 metres. Proceed up **Long Hill** and through the hamlet. Turn right (S) at the first junction in 150 metres and continue straight ahead at the next in 50 metres. Pass the entrance to **Bron Hollow**.

5 In 75 metres we turn left (SE) - opposite the garden of **Rose Cottage** - through a gap in the hedge. A public path follows the hedgerow down to a gate at the asphalt road in 175 metres.

Pre-Jurassic Nyland Hill is a geological island as it pre-dates the great ridge of the Mendip Hills by millions of years.

De Cheddar family brass

6 Turn left (NE) and then right (SSE) in 50 metres, between the bend and **Nethercroft Nurseries**. Cross the pasture, heading to the right of Nyland Hill, and **Landcourse Rhyne** at the footbridge in 200 metres. The path now follows the River Axe, with the rhyne across the to the right, for 600 metres.

Chapel of St Columbanus

7 Turn right (SW), after passing a huge stone projecting from the opposite bank (on the site of a former footbridge) away from the river and into the meadows. Bear left (S) in 175 metres. Keep the rhyne to your right and follow it to **Cocklake** in 600 metres.

8 Turn left (E), beside **Maldon Farm**, along the road to **River House** in 600 metres. Cross **Bartlett's Bridge** and fork left (NW) opposite **Riverside Farm**. This is **Nyland Drove**, a tarred lane across **Monk Moor**, which crosses **Nyland Bridge** in 800 metres. Proceed to **Tor Farm** and **Quarry Farm** in a further 800 metres.

9 Turn right (E), beside Quarry Farm and its delightful garden, and follow the hedgerow around the grassy base of **Nyland Hill** which you can climb for the panoramic view. On the other side of the hillock, in 700 metres, we pass **Rookery Farm** to rejoin the asphalt road through **Nyland** hamlet. Turn right (NE) to **Batt's Farm** and **Court Farm**, followed by **Nyland Stone** hillside outcrop in 400 metres.

Dr Richard Beeching's axe fell on the former Great Western Railway line from Cheddar to Yatton on 1 October 1964 but the 'Strawberry Line' into the town from Cranmore stayed open till 1 April 1969.

Nyland Hill

(10) **Latches Lane** crosses **Dolemead Rhyne** (commemorating a charitable bequest) in 200 metres and leaves the Levels beside **Moor Mead Farm** in a further 200 metres. Continue around the corner in 300 metres to a junction in 75 metres.

(11) Turn left and cross **Draycott Road** - the A371 - in 400 metres. Proceed up **Short Lane** to the junction below Batcombe Farm in 150 metres.

(12) Turn left (NNE) along the **Top Road** and follow it up and over the hill in 1,500 metres. Descend beside **Stone Wood** and **Chapelstone** to **Bradley Cross** in 600 metres. Proceed down **Bradley Cross Lane** for a further 75 metres.

Bradley Cross

(13) Turn left (SW) over a stone stile beside the gate on the corner. Cross the pasture to the kissing gate in 175 metres. Follow the hedgerow (W), together with a power line, into **Froglands Lane** in 400 metres. This is **Cheddar**.

(14) Turn right along **Church Street** and left (W) into **Parson's Pen** in 100 metres. Visit **St Andrew's Church**. At the end of the street, in 150 metres, we go into

an alleyway between **Nos. 4 and 3**. Turn right (N), around the back of **Kings of Wessex School** where you can see the 13th-century ruins of the **Chapel of St Columbanus**. Beside it is the site of the Anglo-Saxon **Palace of Cheddar** and concrete markers in the grass which trace the shape of the Norman **Great Hall**.

Bath Arms Hotel

Cheddar's hexagonal Market Cross, restored in 1887 for Queen Victoria's golden jubilee, was the centrepiece for twice-yearly stock fairs (first Tuesday in May and last Tuesday in October).

15 Turn left (W) along **Bath Street** - away from the Bath Arms Hotel - and also left beside the **War Memorial** at the junction in 150 metres. Follow **Station Road** for 200 metres, passing **Cheddar Court**, and then turn right (NW) into **Valley Line Industrial Park**. In 175 metres, beside **Travis Perkins** we join the **Cheddar Valley Railway Path**. Leave the cycleway after going under **Five Ways Bridge** in 500 metres.

16 Turn left (W) up the steps and turn right beside **Deanside** (W) along **Sharpham Road**. Return to the reservoir car-park in 400 metres.

4 Isle of Wedmore and Blackford

A 7-mile circuit of King Alfred's domain where Guthrum's Danes came to capitulate

Though no longer an island, except when the Levels flood, high ground around Wedmore is the historic cradle of England. It can claim the site of Alfred the Great's villa - the site of which we pass - with star mentions in the Anglo-Saxon Chronicle and contemporary charters. In 878, after the decisive Battle of Edington, surrendered Danish King Guthrum and thirty of his men were brought to Aller, near Langport, where Guthrum was baptised into Christianity. He wore a chrism of white robes and head-cloth for eight days. These were removed at a ceremony in Wedmore which resulted in the 'Peace of Wedmore' and assured the ascendancy of Wessex as the key kingdom that became England. Alfred entertained his former foes at his villa. That is the background to the capital of the Levels. But for Wedmore we would be speaking in a Danish dialect. It is still a place for hospitality in that you will find there are five public houses en route.

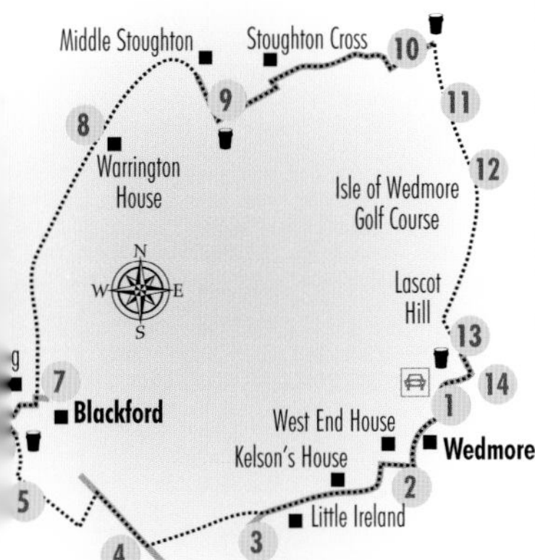

Level:
Length: 7 miles
Terrain: Undemanding and pastoral with plenty of old lanes and no real hills.
Park & start: In **Church Street** at **Wedmore** which is at the intersection of the B3151 from Cheddar and B3139 from Mark.
Start ref.: ST 435 479
Postcode: BS28 4AB
Public transport: Buses from Cheddar to Glastonbury.
Websites: www.sedgemoor.gov.uk www.wedmoreparishcouncil.org.uk:

George Hotel

(1) Set off (W) from the **George Hotel**, uphill through the churchyard, and turn left (S) on the other side in 150 metres. Walk the length of **Granville Road**. Turn right (SW) at the junction in 200 metres, up **Sand Road**, passing **West Hall** and the 1817-dated Wesleyan Chapel which resembles a Byzantine temple. Follow **Sand Road**, for 400 metres, to the second bend.

(2) Turn right (W) into **West End**. Continue straight ahead at the junction beside **Gog's House** in 150 metres. Proceed for a further 50 metres. Turn left (S) opposite **West End House**, into **Plud Street**, and leave the old town at 1890-dated **Kelson's Farm** in 500 metres. Continue straight ahead (W) at the junction and pass the delightfully named **Madwoman's Lane** to the hamlet of **Little Ireland** in 400 metres.

(3) Turn right (WSW) after **Little Ireland House** across the second stile - beside the gate on the corner - and follow the right-hand hedgerow. Keep going straight ahead and cross the stiles into the next two fields. At the end of the third field, in 600 metres, cross into the fourth and final pasture. Go diagonally across it, to the stile beside the gate, in 200 metres.

West End cottage

Wedmore harvest

4 Turn right (NW) along **Wells Way** and walk into **Blackford**. Pass **Hozzard Lane** in 200 metres and continue to **Buckland** in a further 200 metres. Turn left (SSW), opposite the bungalow, into a double-hedged green lane which begins to narrow in 200 metres. Turn right here (NW) through the first of two gates and follow the hedge. **Sexey's School** is to the right.

5 Cross the stile between the gates at the end of the field in 350 metres. Proceed straight ahead, along the farm track, for 50 metres and keep the hedge to your right. Then turn right (N) along the double-hedged dirt lane. Go through the right-hand of the multiple gates in 150 metres and then join the drive to the left of the farmhouse and then the old village school.

6 Turn left (NW) at the road in 150 metres. Pass **Sexey's Arms** and walk down to 1823-dated **Holy Trinity Church** in 200 metres. Turn right (E) along **Church Street** for 250 metres, passing the yucca at **Rose Cottage, Blackford Cottage** dated 1847, and the **Old Vicarage**. Admire the superb sandstone gate pillars at Yew Tree House and the pantiled barn behind.

A pot of 200 silver coins of the 11th-century Danish King Swein Forkbeard and successor Hardacnut – found in the churchyard in 1853 – was acquired by the British Museum.

7 Turn left (N) beside **Tring** and continue straight ahead into a cul-de-sac in 50 metres. Go through the gates into the pasture. The outline of a mediaeval moated manor forms a vague square in the grass to the left. Beyond, in 150 metres, we go through the gate into a double-hedged green lane. Follow it towards the Mendip Hills. Enter a field in 300 metres and follow the left-hand hedgerow straight ahead. The next gate, in 350 metres, brings us into another length of double-hedged track. Brent Knoll is across to the left and Lime Kiln Farm to the right as we head (NE) towards Crook Peak and Ashton Windmill. Emerge from the leafy lane beside the cottage at **Warrington Batch** in 900 metres.

Bishop Giso of Wells acquired the Wedmore royal estate from Edward the Confessor and was granted its church by Queen Matilda, the wife of William the Conqueror.

8 Cross the road and continue straight ahead into the next section of green lane which leads to **Middle Stoughton** in 900 metres. Proceed through the hamlet (SE) to the junction beside the **Hare and Hounds** in 350 metres.

9 Turn left (NE), down to **Stoughton Cross** in 300 metres. Turn left and then right (ENE), in 20 metres, and spot the wayside cross beneath the trees to the left. Pass **Crickham Farm** and the kennels of the Isle of Wedmore Draghounds.

The name Wedmore means 'Hunting Moor' and its early church - precise site unknown - was an Anglo-Saxon Minster.

Brent Knoll skyline

The Abbot of Glastonbury took over much of the ecclesiastical lands and had the tenants in open revolt in 1494, with plans for moorland drainage and enclosure.

The Wedmore memorial to soldier Thomas Hodges, killed in the Siege of Antwerp in 1583, tells of his heart being sent to 'his dear wife in England'.

Imposing porch and tower

10 In 900 metres, at the junction in **Crickham** hamlet we turn right into a double-hedged track (before reaching the **Trotter Inn**). Turn left (ESE) in 6 metres, across a footbridge and stile, and cross the field diagonally to a stile in the top corner in 200 metres. Turn right (S) with a panorama leftwards along the side of the Mendip Hills from Cheddar to Wells and around to Glastonbury Tor. Nyland, rising from the Levels, is the closest hill.

11 In 150 metres, at the top corner of this field, we cross a stile, and then another in 35 metres. Continue straight ahead, keeping the hedge to the left, for 250 metres. Another path comes up the hill from the left and ours turns right and then immediately left to skirt the gate in the corner of the next field facing you. Keep the hedgerow to the left and cross a stile, in 20 metres, to the left of a gate. Resume following the hedge along the ridge to the **Isle of Wedmore Golf Course** in 350 metres.

12 Continue straight ahead - having looked and listened for balls and golfers - to the cut-off end of the hedge on the other side of the fairway in 150 metres. Then turn left and immediately right to keep a dense hedgerow to the left and the greens to the right. Pass above and out of sight of the old Wedmore School. On the other side of the golf links, in 600 metres, we pass through a narrow belt of trees at **Lascot Hill**. Follow the hedge down into **Wedmore** in 400 metres.

13 Turn left (E) along **Manor Road**. The site of Alfred the Great's villa lies between here and the church tower. Walk up to the junction, in 75 metres, where another old school is now the **Village Hall.**

14 Turn right (S) to the **Sun Inn** and the junction in 200 metres. Turn right (W) to return to the **George Inn** in a further 200 metres.

Alfred's villa site at Wedmore

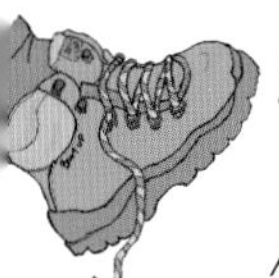

5 Westhay Moor and North Drain

An iconic 5-mile circuit of peatland meres and nature reserves

Level:
Length: 5 miles
Terrain: Well-marked straight tracks across flat ground.
Park & start: In the car-park on **Westhay Moor**, between Peacock Cottage and Lewis's Drove, which is reached by turning off the B3151 at Turnpike House, on the other side of the river from the Bird in Hand.
Start ref.: ST 456 436
Postcode: BA6 9TX
Public transport: None
Websites: www.somersetwildlife.org.uk www.wellstourism.com

Westhay Moor National Nature Reserve is managed by Somerset Wildlife Trust which acquired 247 acres of former peat workings between 1970 and 2002. Being at 4 metres above sea level this was semi-passable ground in prehistoric times, crossed by tracks from the island of Westhay to dry ground towards Wedmore. In the 19th century it had a canal, built by Samuel Galton of Birmingham, between London Drove and Parson's Drove, which brought silt from the River Brue for spreading over peat bogs to turn them into agricultural land. This, however, then sank as the peat deposits compressed and dried. Ground from which peat has been removed has now been turned into a series of dragonfly meres - surrounded by mace-head reeds and splashes of yellow flag-iris and purple loosestrife - which host significant numbers of gadwall, widgeon, shovellor, white goosander and cormorant. Cetti's warbler, hobby, heron and kingfisher are also common.

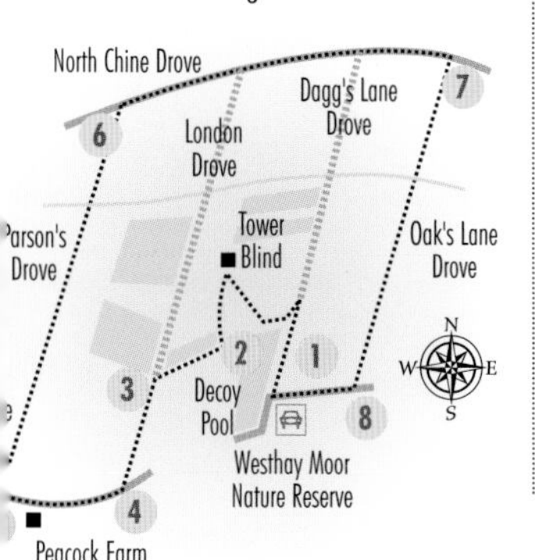

Call of the bittern

1. Set off (N) along **Dagg's Lane Drove** with **Decoy Pool** to the left. Turn left (SW) into grassland beside **Reception Hide** in 400 metres. The first pool and its reed-beds remains to your left. In 150 metres there is a diversionary loop to the right, to **Tower Blind** in 250 metres, which then rejoins the main path in a further 300 metres.

2. Turn right on this path which now passes a second pool, to your right, and joins **London Drove** in 500 metres.

3. Turn left (SSW) to the lane in 600 metres.

Westhay inundated

4. Turn right (W), to the pass the last 200 metres of nature reserve grass and scrub to your right, and then a very modern-looking **Peacock Cottage**. Pass **Peacock Farm** in 200 metres where you cross the rhyne that was **Dalton's Canal**.

5. Turn right (NNE) in 150 metres into **Parson's Drove**. This crosses the **North Drain** in 1,500 metres. In 500 metres it joins a tarred lane as you face the entrance to a rustic smallholding.

6. Turn right (NE) along narrow **North Chine Drove**. This is still at 4 metres above sea level though the Mudgley ridge rises just one pasture away to the left.

From Alfred's time the Kings of England went hawking in the marshes of the Somerset Levels, from royal houses or hunting lodges at Athelney, Axbridge, Cheddar, Glastonbury, Somerton and Wedmore.

(7) Having proceeded along the lane for almost 2,000 metres (and having passed the ends of London Drove and Dagg's Lane Drove) we turn right (SSW) along **Oak's Drove**. Re-cross North Drain in 700 metres. Continue straight ahead to the lane in 1,100 metres.

(8) Turn right (W) to return to the car-park, at the corner, in 400 metres.

A ruckle in the Somerset peatlands was a stack of 1,000 turves but the word passed into history as mechanisation replaced such sights with present-day heaps of black peat.

Otters at Westhay

Sunset from Westhay

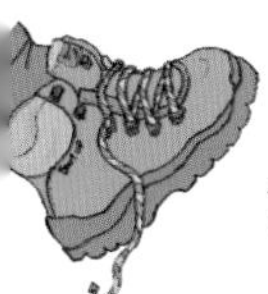

6 Meare and Godney

An 8-mile circuit of the prehistoric Lake Villages below Glastonbury Tor

The alternative ancient Glastonbury centres on its cluster of prehistoric Lake Villages. The first was discovered in March 1892, beside Common Moor and Great Withy Rhyne, by Arthur Bulleid. Excavations continued until 1907. Huts with floors of clay and planks were constructed on wide brushwood platforms that were rafted across what was then marsh and surrounded by palisades. Professor Boyd Dawkins confirmed an Iron Age date. Then a farmer sent a parcel of evidence from two similar but longer used sites north of Oxenpill at Meare. The manors of Meare (2,500 acres), Godney (3,200 acres) and Westhay (1,500 acres) were given to the Abbot of Glastonbury by King Kerelwach of the West Saxons. Now drained, nearby Meare Pool was a 400-acre lagoon, which supplied fish to the Abbey. Meare Fish House and the manorial-style Meare Farm were built by Abbot de Sodbury in about 1300.

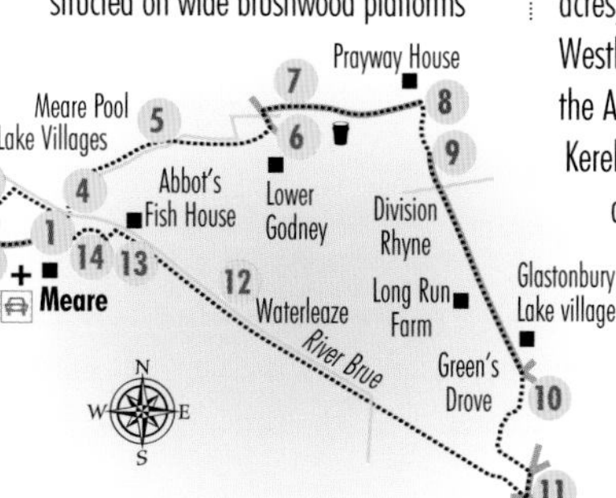

Level:

Length: 8 miles

Terrain: Easy walking, when free of floods, but there are numerous gates and it is common practice to tie-up gates to the extent that they become unopenable. This is no problem for those agile enough to climb over them but it effectively prevents those with any degree of disability from setting out on what would otherwise be a perfect walk across flat country.

Park & start: Approach **Meare** on the B3151 from Glastonbury to Wedmore and park in the vicinity of **St Mary and All Saints' Church**.

Start ref.: ST 455 416

Postcode: BA6 9SJ

Public transport: Buses from Glastonbury to Cheddar.

Websites: www.glastonburytic.co.uk www.mendip.gov.uk/visiting

Swan on the Brue

1 Set off into Meare (W) and pass the war memorial 'to the brave men of this village' in 100 metres. Proceed into **Church Path** - behind the roadside houses - to pass the 1826-built **Congregational Church** and the **Post Office**. Rejoin **St Mary's Road** beside **Stone House** in 300 metres. Continue along the pavement and pass the 1836-dated **Great House**, of three storeys with a rare cast-iron porch. Next is **Meare Manor** with its uplifting inscription: 'Peace on Thy House O passer by.'

2 **Manor Farm** follows, in 400 metres, with a fine cluster of vernacular buildings. Now turn right (N) into **Meareway** and the flat-lands of **Oxenpill**. In 150 metres, from the corner beside **Pound House**, we con-

tinue straight ahead across a stile to the right of the modern barn. Keep straight on over the next stile in 50 metres and another in a further 75 metres. Enter the meadows and head (NE) towards the pylon line and the television transmitter on the Mendip Hills.

3 In 400 metres we come to the embankment beside the **River Brue** and turn right (SE) after having first glanced across the sites of Meare Lake Villages in the meadows down to the left. Follow the bank, through a series of gates, to the triple arches of a stone bridge in 500 metres.

Meare Farm

4 Turn left (N), across the bridge, and go straight ahead through the gate beside the water-trough. Drop down into the meadows and join the track beside the gate in 200 metres. Turn right along the farm track to the bridge across **White's River** and the willow clump in 250 metres.

5 Turn right (NE) on the other side and follow the embankment beside the river. This crosses the historic site of **Meare Pool** fishery. In 300 metres you come to a wartime pillbox that was camouflaged as a barn. Continue straight ahead from it, down to the gate into the corner of the field, in 50 metres. This brings you to the left-hand of three gates.

The Brue at the Fish House

6 Beyond we follow the hedge and the rhyne in the direction of the television mast. In 600 metres, before reaching the corner, turn right through a gate. Then bear left (E) in the field, across a gate in the hedge, in 150 metres. In the next field we continue straight ahead. Follow the hedge to the left-hand of the pair of gates in 400 metres. Then take the right-hand option and follow the farm track into **Lower Godney** in 500 metres.

Wartime pillboxes across the Somerset Levels, constructed during the Battle of Britain, were positioned along rhynes and rivers to form a 'Stop Line', for delaying German Panzers if Hitler had invaded England in 1940.

7 Turn left (NW) in the farm-yard, through the gate, and then left along the asphalt road into the village. Cross the bridge over **James Wear River**, to the junction beside the playing field, in 175

Meare parish church

Godney parish church has been redundant before, having been 'restored to its ancient use' in 1737, and rebuilt in neo-Norman style in 1840 by G. P. Manners, with the chancel apse being added in 1902.

metres. Turn right (E) and pass **Lower Godney House**. Continue straight ahead at the junction in 125 metres. Having passed the **Hawthorns, Oak House** and **Baybrook Farm**, we come in 400 metres to the **Sheppey Inn**. Beyond, after **River Farm**, **Willow Bridge Farm** and **Prayway House**, turn right (S) across a footbridge in 1,000 metres.

Meare war memorial

8 Head for Godney parish church, across the meadows in 450 metres. Services are no longer held but the churchyard remains in use. On the other side the path turns left into a paddock and descends to the road below **Godney Farm** in 50 metres.

9 Turn right (SSE) along **Godney Road**. Cross **Division Rhyne** beside a wartime pillbox in 350 metres. Then in 1,500 metres, in a triangular meadow to the left, we pass marker stones and hollows and humps across the site of **Glastonbury Lake Village**. Continue straight ahead at the junction in 150 metres.

10 Turn right (S) at the next junction in 100 metres. Pass the smallholdings on **Common Moor**. Follow this road (SW) to a junction in 1,100 metres.

Swan sweethearts

11 Turn right here (S), for 175 metres, to approach the **River Brue** and **Meare Road**. Turn right on reaching the stream (NW), across a footbridge, and follow the riverside embankment to **Coldharbour Farm** in 1,500 metres. The path passes the barns, turns right through a gate before the cottage, then immediately right through the next gate. Resume following the embankment in the meadow with the river to your left.

12 In 1,750 metres, after the pastures of **Waterleaze**, we pass the Friesian herd of the **Turnbridge Unit**. Again continue straight ahead. On reaching **Meare** village, in 900 metres, turn left (SW) across the river, into **Porter's Hatch**.

13 Turn right (NW) through the kissing gate in 150 metres.

Abbot's Fish House

Pass **Meare Fish House** and proceed to the gate in front of **Meare Farm** in 250 metres.

14 Turn left and then right around the front of the house, to the churchyard wall in 50 metres. Go through the gate into the farmyard and then turn immediately left (S) into the alleyway beside the graveyard. This returns us to the village street in 100 metres.

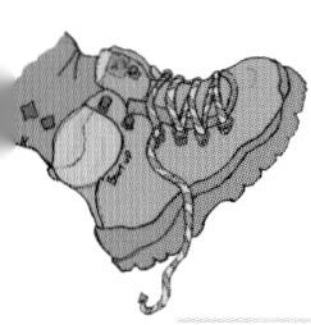

7 Shapwick and Ashcott

An 8-mile circuit into former peat-lands which are reverting to nature

Half of this walk is through nature reserves of one form or another. These are owned by Natural England, the Hawk and Owl Trust and Royal Society for the Protection of Birds. Great expanses of wild land adjoin the Glastonbury Canal. This was built between 1827 and 1833 but was only in use for a generation, being displaced in 1862 by a branch railway of the Somerset and Dorset from Evercreech to Burnham-on-Sea. Poignantly, they run beside each other but both are now disused, unless you count the clusters of birdwatchers and ramblers heading towards the familiar skyline at Glastonbury Tor. The walk starts from the village of Shapwick, which has the Shapwick Hotel, and there is a public house en route - the Railway Inn - beside former Ashcott Station. Veteran railwaymen talk of the time when a steam locomotive came off the line and sank into the peaty canal. Bird twitters are now normal clientele for the district, flocking to news of rarities.

Level:
Length: 8 miles
Terrain: Mostly unpaved tracks but several field paths and a minor slope.
Park & Start: In **Shapwick** village.
Start ref.: ST 418 381
Postcode: TA7 9LP
Public transport: Buses between Bridgwater and Glastonbury.
Websites: www.hawkandowl.org.uk www.naturalengland.org.uk

Heron and flying fish

Excavations along the line of the Sweet Track show that it ran for two kilometres from the Polden Hills to an island of firm ground between Westhay and Meare.

1 Set off (W) from the cross-roads beside the south side of **St Mary's Church**. This was built in 1330. Proceed along **Church Road** and pass **The Courtyard** and **Mill Lane**.

2 Turn right (N) after the **Old Barn** in 200 metres and bear left (NW) in 150 metres into **Kent Lane**. Follow this to **Kent Farm** in 1,000 metres.

3 Turn right (NNE) after **Aston Hall** and **Springs Barn** in 150 metres. This is **Kent Drove**, initially downhill, which then goes up and over a rise in 1,000 metres, into pastures which were acquired by the Hawk and Owl Trust in 2007. Continue straight ahead across **Shapwick Moor** to gates on the slope in 500 metres. Enter **Shapwick Heath National Nature Reserve**. Stay on the main track. This passes between a delightful mixture of hay pastures, peat meres and damp scrubby woodland.

Shapwick Heath Nature Reserve

4 In 500 metres, the main track turns sharply right (SE) into **Head Drove** which passes **Canada Farm** and leads to **Station Road** in 800 metres.

5 Turn left (NNE) to the bridge in 700 metres beside the site of **Shapwick Station** on the former branch railway from Glastonbury to Bridgwater and Burnham.

6 Turn right (SE) along the old railway line on a causeway beside the earlier **Glastonbury Canal**. This is to your left. In 200 metres, to the right, a track and boardwalk follow the sunken remains of the Sweet Track which is 5,817-years-old. The branches of an 'X' shaped frame and the hurdle-like walkway it supported lie in the peat where a pipe runs above in order to provide water to keep them saturated during drought years. Otherwise the prehistoric timbers would dry out and disintegrate. In a further 1,800 metres there is a much more recent track to the left (N) across a bridge, to the hide beyond the trees which looks across the marshes of **Mere Heath**. Alternatively, to the right (S), the waterside path leads to **Noah's Hide**. You stand a reasonable chance of seeing otters on a quiet day.

Little egret over the marshes

Glastonbury Canal

Kent Drove

7 In 1,000 metres the canal-side track brings us to **Ashcott Corner** and former **Ashcott Station**. The **Railway Inn** is to the left and the track across the road runs through **Ham Wall National Nature Reserve**. Our onward route turns right (SSW) to **Buscott Farm** at the cross-roads in 1,400 metres.

Canada Farm ditch

8 Turn right (NW) along **Buscott Lane** to the sharp corner in 500 metres.

9 Turn left (SW) at the gates on the bend. Follow the hedgerow oaks up the slope for 250 metres. Continue straight ahead (S), with **Buscott Copse** to your left, into the corner of the arable field in 400 metres. Turn right (W), staying inside the same field, for 175 metres. Now turn left (S) across the footbridge, to cross the source of **Cats Drove Stream**.

Autumn and winter flocks of tens of thousands of starlings gather around the woods at Shapwick towards dusk and put down in the reed beds to roost for the night.

Buscott Farm harvest

(10) Go up the slope, beside the hedgerow, across two pastures, to a gate beside the trees near the corner in 300 metres. Turn right (SW), through the gate, and then fork right (WNW) in 15 metres. **Millslade Hill** and its buildings are up to the left. Our double-hedged track enters pastures. Then follow the hedgerow straight ahead, into another stub-end of green lane, to a road in 1,000 metres.

Acidic anaerobic conditions of permanently sodden peat make this the perfect medium for preserving bone, leather, pollen and wood, though all of these soon decay and deteriorate on exposure to the air.

(11) Turn right (NW), along the lane, to the sharp corner in 500 metres. Leave the road by continuing straight ahead (W) into arable land. Follow the hedgerow to **Shapwick**, to the gate into **Vicarage Lane**, in 350 metres. This brings us to a road junction in 150 metres.

(12) Turn right (N), along **Main Street**, into the centre of the village in 200 metres.

The Sweet Track (named for peat-digger Raymond Sweet who found it in 1970) has been dated by its tree-rings to 3806 or 3807 BC in the Neolithic period - making it the oldest-known road in Europe.

Heron in-flight reflection

8 Burrow Mump and Southlake Moor

A five-mile walk from an iconic hilltop around meadows that become a huge winter bird-lake

Lapwing, snipe and woodcock are the principal breeding birds across Southlake Moor which was one of the first of the levels to be reclaimed from reed-beds and converted to meadows. An area of 485 acres, now a site of special scientific interest, reverts to a wetland in winter. It becomes one of the biggest bird lakes in England with thousands of widgeon, pochard, tufted duck and teal and Bewick's swan. Overlooking it, conical Burrow Mump is an iconic silhouette of the Somerset Levels, with vestiges of Anglo-Saxon and Norman fortifications plus an archetypal romantic ruin. The tower of the mediaeval church was restored in 1724 but the repair project was then abandoned. Burrow Mump was given to the nation in 1946 by Major Barrett: 'This hill was given to the National Trust by Alexander Gould Barrett that the men and women of Somerset who died serving their country in the Second World War may be remembered here in time to come.'

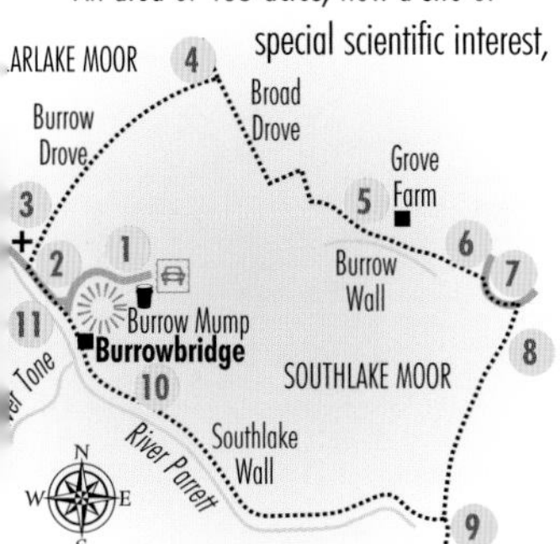

Level:
Length: 5 miles
Terrain: Unstrenuous and hopefully uneventful provided you do not venture out into a flood or if the puddles are hard-frozen by winter frosts.
Park &start: From the National Trust car-park below **Burrow Mump** at **Burrowbridge**, beside the A361, on the Othery side of the hill.
Start ref.: ST 360 306
Postcode: TA7 0RB
Public transport: Buses from Bridgwater to Langport.
Websites:
www.nationaltrust.org.uk/wessex
www.rickladt@onetel.com

Sluices on the Parrett

1 Set off up and over the hill (SW) through the ruins of **St Michael's Church** in 175 metres and then bear right (W) towards **Burrowbridge Primary School** and descend into the village via a flight of steps in 100 metres. Turn left (W) along the **Main Road**, passing **Hillside Cottage**, cross into **School Lane** in 50 metres. In 75 metres you come to a junction at **Swallows**.

2 Turn right (N), along **Riverside**, with your back to the inn and the generally turbid **River Parrett** to the left. Pass the lorry depot of **Gillard's Transport** and the mellow brickwork of **Dyke House**. Approach the barns at **Samways Farm** in 200 metres.

An Act of Parliament in 1830 allowed the Southlake Moor to be 'warped' over each winter by three to four feet of controlled floodwater to protect the grass from frost, cause silt deposition, and bring on a lush expanse of early grass.

Male stonechat in the reeds

(3) Just before reaching them, turn right (NE), down into **Burrow Drove**. Pass two pairs of council-built homes and cross **Earlake Moor**. In 1,500 metres you come to a T-junction with another grassy drove.

(4) Turn right (SSE) and keep a distant Barrow Mump to your right. Head back towards the main road. Fork left (SE) on approaching **Burrow Wall Farm** in 750 metres.

Earlake Moor photocall

Southlake Moor

(5) Cross the **A361**, in 200 metres, to the public path on the other side. In just 30 metres this turns left, through the first gate, and follows the stout 6-feet high earth-work of **Burrow Wall** as it bends to the right of **Grove Farm** in 200 metres. Henceforth, for the remainder of the walk, **Southlake Moor** is to your right. The path takes you beneath power cables and then follows the foot of the escarpment which is smothered with elm scrub. Cross the stile at the fence in 350 metres.

Northern slopes

Romantic ruin

6 Continue straight ahead, following the left-hand fence to the first corner of this pasture, in 150 metres. Head for **Pathe Barn**, and go through two gates - the first to the left of the garden and the next beside the barn itself.

7 Turn right along the asphalt road in 100 metres and follow it around the series of bends. In 250 metres you reach a road junction just before **Byways Cottage**.

Southlake Moor, one of the lowest of the levels, was drained for the Abbot of Glastonbury between 1255 and 1262, behind an embankment known as Burrow Wall.

The Parrett beside Southlake Wall

8 Turn right, for 10 metres, to cross the bridge. Then turn right again (SW) on to a path beside the ditch. Next it crosses a metal foot-bridge and follows a rhyne. Continue straight ahead, through the gates, towards the next hamlet. Climb on to the embankment beside an outlying cottage, in 1,200 metres, and go through the gate immediately opposite the gable-end of the building.

9 Turn right (W) to follow **Southlake Wall** above the **River Parrett** along a permissive path which provides a scenic section for two long-distance routes (being shared by Macmillan Way West and East Deane Way). Keep the river and the hamlets of **Stathe** and **Warmoor** across to your left. You can glimpse the double gables of 1929-dated Stathe Sunday School and Jubilee Chapel (named for Queen Victoria's 50 years in 1887). There is also a delicensed King William Inn, in Warmoor, with its name just readable in roadside brickwork.

Steam pumps to drain Southlake Moor, installed between 1845 and 1869, were replaced by diesel pumps in 1948.

The King Alfred

10 In 2,000 metres we reach the confluence of the Parrett with the **River Tone** from Taunton. Proceed (NW) into **Burrowbridge** in 300 metres. The bridge has an 1814-stone to builder John Stone from Yarcombe in Devon (though the parish then belonged to Dorset).

11 Turn right (E) at the junction beside the **King Alfred Inn**. Also pass the replacement **St Michael's Church**, an exceedingly bland building, dating from 1836.

Make sure you turn right in 100 metres, after **Hillside Cottage**, so you are inside the **Burrow Mump** hedge (rather than risk the dangerous bend in the road) to return to the car-park in 250 metres.

Burrow Mump

Burrow Mump is top contender for the site of King Alfred's marching camp at Easter 878 before the decisive Battle of Edington over the Danes, near Westbury, Wiltshire.

The earliest recorded name of Burrow Mump was 'Tutte-yate', before its entrenchment with timber palisades, for a Norman castle.

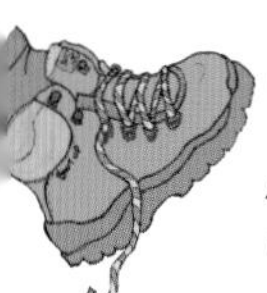

9 Somerton and Dundon

A 9-mile circuit from an historic town, via a couple of nature reserve hilltops

Dundon Beacon dominates this walk, with the same molehill profile as Brent Knoll, though it is largely tree-covered. The summit, however, has been partially cleared to provide niches for rock rose, musk mallow, common milkwort, stinking iris and autumn ladies tresses. Birdsfoot trefoil colonises old anthills. Much different in character, with better views due to the absence of trees, is Lollover Hill. Its signs proclaim a site of special scientific interest, listed by English Nature, and a delightful green lane heads for Dundon village. In a way the best of the hills is the smallest, of lithe Cinderella shape and size. This is West Hill, between Dundon and the cul-de-sac hamlet of Littleton. Bradley Hill overlooks Somerton and Gilling Hill has naked geology, exposed from grey through to red, more like a sea-cliff than an inland slope. It used to look down on the ancient shore when the Somerset Levels were inundated by the sea and winter floods.

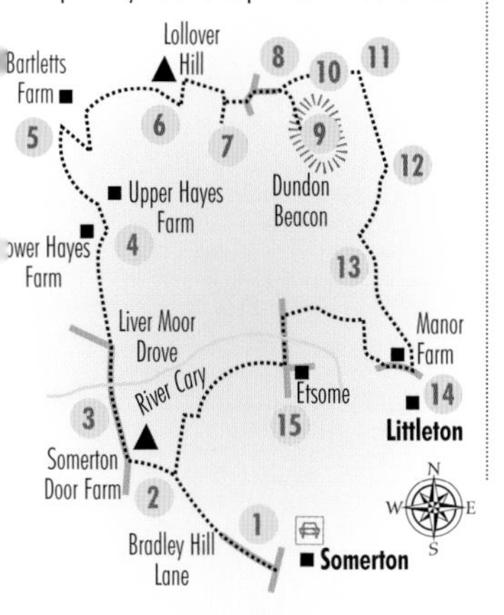

Level:
Terrain: Simple walking, apart from two or three climbs, though one is optional
Length: 9 miles
Park & start: Midway along **Northfield** in **Somerton** between **Langport Road** to the south and **Etsome Road** to the north.
Start ref.: ST 483 289
Postcode: TA11 6SL
Public transport: Buses from Langport to Street.
Websites:
www.somerton-t.c@tiscali.co.uk
www.southsomerset.gov.uk

River Cary

1 Set off (NW) into **Bradley Hill Lane** which becomes a dirt track at the top of the hill and descends to a junction with **Somerset Door Drove** in 1,500 metres.

2 Turn right (N) along this road to pass the stone-mullioned farmhouse and corrugated iron buildings at **Somerset Door**. Cross the **River Cary** at **Somerset Door Bridge** in 600 metres. Proceed to the corner in 300 metres.

The site of ancient Somerton Castle is around the White Hart Hotel which can claim original Norman masonry and vaults for its foundations.

3 Here we leave the road and continue straight ahead into **Liver Moor Drove**. Cross the meadows and rhynes to **Lower Hayes** in 1,000 metres. Having turned left and then right through the farmyard, we come to a house and bend in the road at the entrance to **Upper Hayes Farm** in 125 metres.

4 Turn left here (NW), across the stile in the far corner of the garden, and cross the lawn. Keep the hedgerow to your right and cross the next stile into the paddocks and fields. Continue to keep the same hedge immediately to your right for 600 metres.

Conservation grazers, Lollover Hill

Somerton, the first capital of Wessex, has its mention in the Anglo-Saxon Chronicle, as a 'royal vill' occupied by Aethelbald in 733.

5 On entering the field before reaching **Bartlett's Farm** we bear right and walk up to the gate in the top corner of the hillside pasture in 250 metres. This pasture is criss-crossed by three public paths and has the hummocks of mediaeval strip fields. Follow the hedge (N) in the next field and bear right in 150 metres (NE), keeping the hedgerow to your left, to the stile in 175 metres. Continue straight ahead, to enter access land on **Lollover Hill** in 600 metres, with **Park Wood** to your left.

6 Bear right (SE) for 150 metres, to climb to the Ordnance Survey triangulation pillar on the summit, which at 290 feet above sea level has a panoramic view from Glastonbury Tor to the railway viaduct at Somerton. Descend (NE) towards Park Wood and the Tor to the gate and stile in 200 metres. Grassy and double-hedged **Lollover Lane** drops (ESE) towards Dundon village. In 400 metres it bends to the right (S).

7 Turn left (E) just 20 metres after the corner. A narrow footpath between hedges takes us into **Dundon** in 100 metres. We emerge on the corner opposite **Lollover Thatch**. For a worthwhile diversion, **St Andrew's Church** is up a cul-de-sac to the left, with a huge yew tree having a girth of ten feet. Inside the church has a Jacobean raised pulpit, up six steps, which is set into the wall.

Church Farm triangle

8 Our walk continues up to the left from **Little Thatch**, for 40 metres, to the next junction where we bear right between triangular-plan **Church Farm** and **Spring Cottage**. This is **School Lane** which passes **Compton Dundon Primary School** and brings us to a grassy track which bends to the right in 300 metres.

St Andrew's Church at Dundon stands beside a huge yew tree, and has a Jacobean raised pulpit, up six steps and set in a wall.

Dundon Hill

9 Here we have another optional diversion, up through **Hillwall Wood** to **Dundon Beacon Nature Reserve**, which is managed by Somerset Wildlife Trust. The stony rampart of an Iron Age hill-fort encircles the plateau in 350 metres. Beyond, in 400 metres, the tree-topped beacon - at 335 feet above sea level - looks across to the Hood Monument, commemorating the famous Admiral.

10 On returning the 750 metres to the stile and gate at the bottom of the hill we proceed for a further 7 metres. Turn right (NE) through the kissing gate and follow the dense hedgerow, keeping it to your left, and ignore any stile or opening in it. In 200 metres we bear right (E), still keeping the hedge to our left, and Hillwall Beacon and Dundon Beacon across to the right. Castlebrook and the Hood Monument are over to the left. Head towards Gilling Down and the exposed geology of the slopes that give name to Redland below.

Llama at Littleton

11 In 500 metres, at the end of third pasture, we turn right (S). Gilling Down is now to the left and Dundon Beacon on the right. Cross the stile in each corner of the fields and follow the hedge to **Peak Lane** in 800 metres.

12 Turn left and then immediately right, in 10 metres, to cross into a double-hedged green lane. This brings us to an orchard in 100 metres. Keep the hedge to the left and apple trees to the right. In 300 metres, cross a stile and ditch, and keep the hedge to the right. It gradually bears right (SW) into flatter ground.

13 Turn left (S) in 250 metres, behind the oak tree in the same field (ignoring another stile further to the left). Head up and over **West Hill**, for 800 metres, and then descend into **Littleton** hamlet in 300 metres. Keep Manor Farm to the right and the main road to the right as you walk down to a stile beneath cypress trees to the left of a modern house. Cross the lawn to the gate into the lane opposite **Westville House**.

Turn right (W), away from the B3151 on **Littleton Hill**. Follow the lane around to the right (N) in 250 metres between **Bartlett's Cottage** and **Charity Cottage**. Pass **Summerleigh** and follow the unpaved lane for 600 metres. Turn left (W), along an unfenced farm road, to **Etsome** in 750 metres. Turn left (S) along the road through the hamlet and re-cross the **River Cary** at **Etsome Bridge** in 200 metres.

Dundon Beacon, with its mediaeval beacon mound set on the rampart of an Iron Age hill-fort, is managed by Somerset Wildlife Trust.

Somerton

Continue straight ahead at the junction, in 100 metres, up **Etsome Hill** for a further 200 metres. Turn right (W) into double-hedged **Grove Lane**. This bridleway gradually bends to the left (SW) to follow the foot of a semi-wooded hill-side. Turn right and then left at a kink in 800 metres. Hereon the track is much narrower. In 400 metres it climbs a slope and emerges on the muddy section of **Bradley Hill Lane**. Turn left, uphill, to return to **Somerton** in 1,000 metres.

10 Muchelney and Thorney

A 5-mile circuit around the former 'Great Island' that abounds with ecclesiastical relics

Level:
Length: 5 miles
Terrain: Causeways, pastures and lanes around the flood-plain (which still lives up to its name).
Park & start: In the ancient end of **Muchelney**, approached from Langport, in the vicinity of the **Toll House** and **Almonry Farm**.
Start ref.: ST 429 250
Postcode: TA10 0DF
Public transport: Buses from Langport to Martock.
Websites:
www.english-heritage.org.uk/muchelney
www.johnleachpottery.co.uk

For 600 years, from Anglo-Saxon times, Muchelney Abbey was the great religious house of the Somerset Levels. When confiscated by Henry VIII and granted to Edward Seymour, Earl of Hertford, its lands were regarded as cursed. Elevated to Duke of Somerset and Protector of England, Seymour would lose his head for treason on 22 January 1552. History abounds in this quiet place. It used to be much busier. The Toll House shows that the mediaeval road system, drawn to the bustle and business surrounding the Benedictine monastery, continued in importance into the turnpike era. Firm ground around the village, between the rivers Parrett and Yeo, was known as 'the Great Island'. Being only 25 feet above sea level, and less than that above the River Parrett, flooded meadows and roads can easily restore Muchelney to its historic status as an island. You will then need a boat or helicopter to complete the walk.

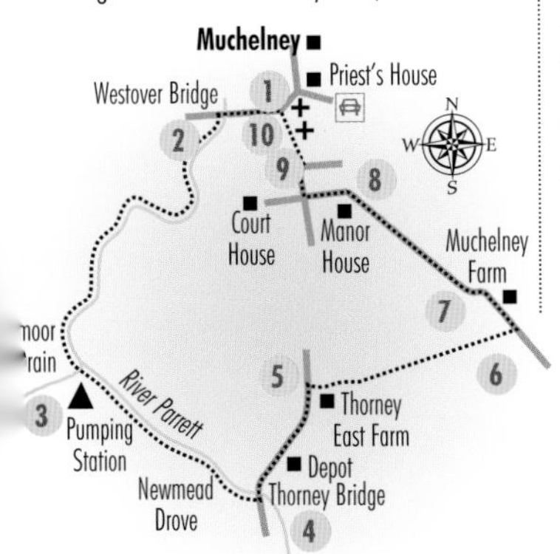

1 Set off from the cross and triangle of grass between the **Church of St Peter and St Paul** and the thatched **Priest's House** which is owned by the National Trust. Turn towards Drayton and Curry Rivel. Pass the **Almonry** and **Abbot's House**, next to the extensive floor-plan view of **Muchelney Abbey**. Turn left in 150 metres to visit the Benedictine survivals if your visit coincides with English Heritage opening hours. Our onward route along the road (W) is to **Wendover Bridge** in 300 metres.

The Priest's House, a 14th-century glebe house used by secular priests serving the parish church, was acquired by the National Trust in 1911.

Priest's House

Pumping Station

2 Cross the bridge and turn left (SW) across a stile beside the gate. Keep the **River Parrett** to your left. The embankment retains and rises above winter floodwater. In 500 metres we cross a lesser causeway, no longer with a bridge, which carried the former branch railway from Yeovil and Martock to Langport West and the West of England mainline at Curry Rivel Junction. Proceed for 1,500 metres, crossing a succession of stiles at gates and rhynes. The embanked path swings to the right on approaching a **Pumping Station** to take you above and around a complex of older sluice-gates.

Village sign

3 Turn left (SE) to cross **Southmoor Main Drain** and its weirs. Continue to follow the **Parrett Trail** which bends to the left along the access road to the Pumping Station. Fork left to pass directly beside triple outlets. Bear left on the other side to cross older sluices of **Westmoor Main Drain** which heads towards Barrington. Then bear right and resume following the embanked western side of the River Parrett, for 1,500 metres, to **Thorney Bridge**.

4 Turn left (N), along the road, and pass John Budge's haulage yard at **Thorney Transport Depot** to go over the old railway bridge in 300 metres. In 250 metres, after **Thorney Lakes**, the road bends to the left at Granary Barn. It then bends to the right, after **Thorney East Farm** and opposite a farmyard in 150 metres.

Westover Bridge

Rhynes and rivers surround the village

5 Here we turn right (E), before reaching the thatched Muchelney Pottery, into a dirt lane which passes **Waggon House** in 75 metres. This becomes a public path over the rise and into the meadows. After a length of green lane we fork left, beside the willows at an embanked lake, where you will probably see more ducks and geese and a heron. Beyond it we proceed straight ahead, to cross **Prior Brook**, 500 metres from Thorney.

6 At the end of the field we go through a gate and follow the hedgerow straight ahead. Keep the hedge to your right. **Daws Farm** is across to the left. At the end of this field, 350 metres from the bridge, we turn right and then left. Now keep the woody hedgerow to your left and follow it towards the pantiled frontage of mullioned **Muchelney Ham Farm** in 300 metres.

7 Turn left (NW), along the road through **Muchelney Ham** hamlet, to another ancient wall at **North Ham Farm**, to **Muchelney** village in 1,300 metres.

Tudor costumes and slogan-style messages date the flying angels on a blue-sky background across the barrel-vaulted ceiling of the parish church to early in the 17th century.

Broken railway

8 Turn left (W) after the **Manor House** to the cross-roads at the junction in 250 metres. Turn right (N) here, though devotees of ancient buildings can divert left and then right to see mediaeval Court House at the end of the cul-de-sac. Spot the wall-mounted Automobile Association roundel at the cross-roads.

9 Our onward road brings us to a corner in 200 metres. Go straight ahead, over fence bars and across the field, to enter the farmyard in a further 200 metres.

King Athelstan, grandson of Alfred the Great, founded (or re-founded) the Anglo-Saxon Abbey at Muchelney in 939 AD.

10 The public path exits through the wooden gate to the left of Abbot's House and the English Heritage entrance. A grassy path returns us to the road beside the steps to the immense but flattened **Abbey Church** which stretches across to the rather more modest people's church in 200 metres.

Ruins of the Abbey Church, set in a huge lawn, are 216 feet in length and 52 feet in width and the chunky foundations extend into the adjoining churchyard.

Court House